D1161168

Super
SAINT BERNARDS

STRONG! INTELLIGENT! DIGNIFIED!

GENTLE! OBEDIENT! LOYAL!

ABDO
Publishing Company

Mary Elizabeth Salzmann

Consulting Editor, Diane Craig, M.A./Reading Specialist

Published by ABDO Publishing Company
8000 West 78th Street, Edina, Minnesota 55439.

Printed in the United States of America,
North Mankato, Minnesota
052010
092010

 PRINTED ON RECYCLED PAPER

Editor: Katherine Hengel
Content Developer: Nancy Tuminelly
Cover and Interior Design and Production:
    Anders Hanson, Mighty Media
Illustrations: Bob Doucet
Photo Credits: Mary Bloom, Shutterstock

Library of Congress Cataloging-in-Publication Data
Salzmann, Mary Elizabeth, 1968-
  Super Saint Bernards / by Mary Elizabeth Salzmann ;
illustrated by Bob Doucet.
    p. cm. -- (Dog daze)
  ISBN 978-1-61613-381-8
1. Saint Bernard dog--Juvenile literature. I. Doucet, Bob, ill.
II. Title.
  SF429.S3S87 2011
  636.73--dc22
                    2010002395

Super SandCastle™ books are created by a team of professional
educators, reading specialists, and content developers around
five essential components—phonemic awareness, phonics,
vocabulary, text comprehension, and fluency—to assist young
readers as they develop reading skills and strategies and
increase their general knowledge. All books are written,
reviewed, and leveled for guided reading, early reading
intervention, and Accelerated Reader® programs for use in
shared, guided, and independent reading and writing activities to
support a balanced approach to literacy instruction.

CONTENTS

BODY BASICS

Size

Saint Bernards are 25 to 28 inches (64 to 71 cm) tall. They weigh 130 to 180 pounds (59 to 82 kg).

Build

Saint Bernards are tall, strong, and muscular. They have powerful necks and wide shoulders.

Tail

A Saint Bernard's tail is long and heavy. The end is wide and turns up slightly.

Legs and Feet

Saint Bernards have muscular legs. Their feet are wide, and they have strong toes.

5

COAT & COLOR

Saint Bernard Fur

Saint Bernards can have short or long hair. Short coats are **dense** and smooth. The fur is longer on the thighs and the base of the tail. Long coats can be slightly wavy, but not curly. Long-haired Saint Bernards have bushy tails.

The Saint Bernard's coat is white with patches of color. Common colors are red, brown, orange, and **brindle**. The chest, feet, **muzzle**, neck, and tip of the tail are usually white. The face and ears are often black.

BROWN FUR

WHITE AND BROWN COAT

Saint Bernards come in many different colors and coats.
The photos on these pages show just a few examples.

RED FUR

ORANGE FUR

BLACK FUR

RED AND WHITE COAT

ORANGE AND WHITE COAT

BRINDLE AND WHITE COAT

HEALTH & CARE

Life Span

Most Saint Bernards live about 8 to 10 years.

Grooming

All Saint Bernards **shed**. They shed the most in the spring and fall. They should be brushed often. They also drool a lot. Use rags to wipe their mouths.

VET'S CHECKLIST

- Have your Saint Bernard spayed or neutered. This will prevent unwanted puppies.

- Visit a vet for regular check-ups.

- Ask your vet about which foods are right for your Saint Bernard.

- Clean your Saint Bernard's teeth and ears once a week.

- Make sure your Saint Bernard gets enough exercise.

- Brush your Saint Bernard at least once a week.

EXERCISE & TRAINING

Activity Level

Saint Bernards are not very energetic. When they are full grown, they are calm. But they need regular exercise. They should go on long walks a few times a week. Otherwise, they can have problems with their bones and joints.

Obedience

Training is very important for Saint Bernards because of their size. An untrained Saint Bernard might break things or hurt someone. Luckily, they are smart and like to please people. They learn quickly and are good at following rules. It's a good idea to start training early.

A Few Things You'll Need

A **leash** lets your Saint Bernard know that you are the boss. With a leash, you can guide your dog where you want it to go. Most cities require that dogs be on leashes when they are outside.

A **collar** is a strap that goes around your Saint Bernard's neck. You can attach a leash to the collar to take your dog on walks. You should also attach an **identification tag** with your home address. If your dog ever gets lost, people will know where it lives.

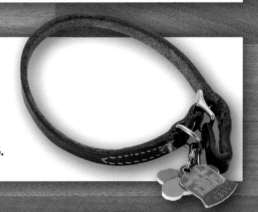

Toys keep your dog healthy and happy. Dogs like to chase and chew on them.

A **dog bed** will help your pet feel safe and comfortable at night.

ATTITUDE & INTELLIGENCE

Personality

Well-trained Saint Bernards are friendly. Saint Bernards are patient and gentle with children. They are loyal and protective of family members.

Intellect

Saint Bernards are very smart dogs. They learn new things quickly. They have been trained as watchdogs, rescue dogs, and herding dogs. They can even learn to pull carts!

All About Me

Hi! My name is Ben. I'm a Saint Bernard. I just wanted to let you know a few things about me. I made some lists below of things I like and dislike. Check them out!

Things I Like

- Going on walks
- Being with my family
- Relaxing on the couch
- Playing with kids
- Pleasing people

Things I Dislike

- Staying outside all day
- Being left alone
- Not getting enough exercise
- Being too hot

LITTERS & PUPPIES

Litter Size

Female Saint Bernards can give birth to up to 12 puppies.

Diet

Newborn pups drink their mother's milk. Saint Bernards can begin to eat soft puppy food when they are about four weeks old.

Growth

Saint Bernards should stay with their mothers until they are about eight weeks old. Saint Bernards can take up to three years to become full grown.

BUYING A SAINT BERNARD

Choosing a Breeder

It's best to buy a puppy from a **breeder**, not a pet store. When you visit a dog breeder, ask to see the mother and father of the puppies. Make sure the parents are healthy, friendly, and well behaved.

Picking a Puppy

Choose a puppy that isn't too **aggressive** or too shy. If you crouch down, some of the puppies may want to play with you. One of them might be the right one for you!

16

Is It the Right Dog for You?

Buying a dog is a big decision. You'll want to make sure your new pet suits your lifestyle.

Get out a piece of paper. Draw a line down the middle.

Read the statements listed here. Each time you agree with a statement from the left column, make a mark on the left side of your paper. When you agree with a statement from the right column, make a mark on the right side of your paper.

Left			Right
I like to take long walks.	☐	☐	I don't like to walk.
I want to work on training my dog.	☐	☐	I don't want a dog that needs a lot of training.
I have a fenced-in yard.	☐	☐	I don't have a fenced-in yard.
I enjoy brushing my dog.	☐	☐	I don't like to have to brush my dog.
I don't mind dog drool.	☐	☐	I think dog drool is disgusting!
I want to spend time with my dog.	☐	☐	I want a dog that doesn't need a lot of attention.
I don't mind having a lot of dog fur to clean up.	☐	☐	I don't want to have to clean up a lot of dog fur.

If you marked more X's on the left side than on the right side, a Saint Bernard may be the right dog for you! If you have more X's on the right side of your paper, you might want to consider another breed.

17

GIANTS OF THE ALPS

Saint Bernards are from Switzerland. They were **bred** from large dogs brought there by the Romans. Because of their strength, they could pull carts. They were also used as watchdogs and herders.

The Saint Bernard **breed** got its name in the 1600s. That's when they were first brought to a **hospice** in the Swiss Alps. It was run by monks who helped people traveling through the mountains. The monks discovered that the dogs could find their way during snowstorms. And they were very good at finding people buried in deep snow. The Saint Bernards at the hospice have saved more than 2,000 people.

Bernard of Menthon was a priest who started the hospice in 1050. He later became known as Saint Bernard. The hospice and the dogs were both named after him.

Tails of Lore
BARRY TO THE RESCUE!

Barry was
a Saint Bernard
who lived at the
hospice from 1800
to 1812. During his life, he
saved more than 40 people.

One of the people Barry saved was a young boy.
The boy was on an icy ledge in a snowstorm. It was
too **dangerous** for a person to climb up to rescue the boy.

FACIAL FEATURES

Head

Saint Bernards have large, wide heads with short **muzzles**. Their foreheads have wrinkles.

Teeth and Mouth

A Saint Bernard can have a scissors bite or an even bite.

Eyes

Saint Bernards have medium-sized, brown eyes. The lower eyelids may not close completely.

Ears

A Saint Bernard's ears stick out a little at the base. They hang down along the head.

4

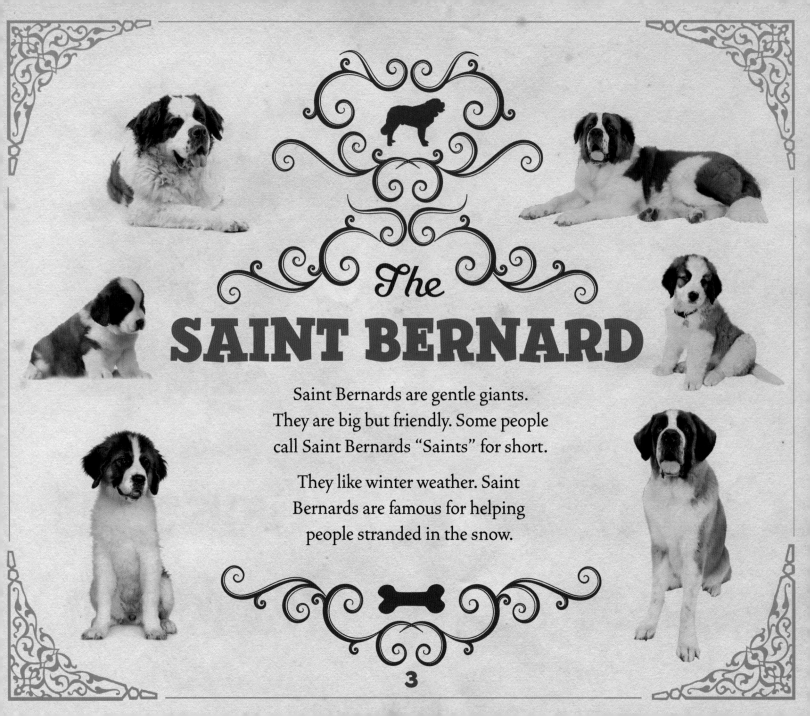

The
SAINT BERNARD

Saint Bernards are gentle giants. They are big but friendly. Some people call Saint Bernards "Saints" for short.

They like winter weather. Saint Bernards are famous for helping people stranded in the snow.

But Barry was able to get to the ledge. He licked the boy's face until he woke up. The boy wrapped his arms around Barry's neck and held on tight. Barry carried the boy to safety!

Barry's body is in the Natural History Museum in Bern, Switzerland. And there is a statue of him at the pet **cemetery** in Paris, France.

FIND THE
SAINT BERNARD

A

B

C

D

THE SAINT BERNARD QUIZ

1. Saint Bernards have wrinkles on their foreheads. **True or false?**

2. Saint Bernards have long tails. **True or false?**

3. Saint Bernards are very energetic. **True or false?**

4. Saint Bernards are gentle with children. **True or false?**

5. Saint Bernards are from England. **True or false?**

6. Barry saved a young boy from a fire. **True or false?**

Answers: 1) true 2) true 3) false 4) true 5) false 6) false

GLOSSARY

aggressive - likely to attack or confront.

breed - 1. to raise animals that have certain traits. A *breeder* is someone whose job is to breed certain animals. 2. a group of animals with common ancestors.

brindle - a pattern of dark streaks or spots.

cemetery - a place where dead people or pets are buried.

dangerous - able or likely to cause harm or injury.

dense - thick or crowded together.

hospice - a hotel, usually one run by a religious group.

muzzle - an animal's nose and jaws.

shed - to lose something, such as skin, leaves, or fur, through a natural process.

DATE DUE

			PRINTED IN U.S.A.